MW00934888

Contents

Chapter 1: Introduction: The Thrill of the Hunt

The allure of treasure hunting is timeless. From childhood stories of pirates searching for buried gold to modern-day expeditions for lost artifacts, the idea of discovering something extraordinary has always captivated the human imagination. But what is it about the prospect of treasure that sparks such excitement? Is it the promise of wealth, the challenge of the unknown, or something deeper—a quest for meaning, adventure, and self-discovery?

This chapter serves as a gateway to understanding the core of treasure hunting, both literal and metaphorical. It explores why we are drawn to the idea of hidden treasures, the transformative power of the journey, and how embarking on a treasure hunt can enrich our lives in unexpected ways.

The Universal Fascination with Treasure

The concept of treasure is as old as humanity itself. From ancient myths of lost civilizations to legends like the Holy Grail or Atlantis, stories of hidden riches have been passed down through generations. These tales often symbolize more than material wealth; they represent dreams, hopes, and the ultimate reward for perseverance and courage.

As children, we were enthralled by tales of pirates with maps marked by an "X" that promised gold-filled chests. As adults, we are still drawn to the excitement of the chase—whether it's searching for rare collectibles, exploring family heirlooms, or uncovering long-lost history. Treasure hunting taps into a primal instinct: the desire to explore, to conquer the unknown, and to uncover secrets waiting to be revealed.

Why We Hunt: The Psychology Behind the Search

The thrill of treasure hunting isn't just about the reward; it's also about the process. Psychologists suggest that the act of seeking activates a part of our brain tied to curiosity and satisfaction. The joy of uncovering something hidden, of solving a mystery, fuels a deep sense of accomplishment.

Treasure hunting also provides an escape from the mundane. In a world where daily routines can feel monotonous, the hunt offers a chance to break free, to embark on an adventure that promises surprises and challenges at every turn. Whether you're searching for physical riches or intangible rewards like personal growth, the pursuit itself is exhilarating.

The Real Treasures of Life

While the idea of finding gold, gems, or rare artifacts is enticing, the true treasures of life often lie elsewhere. They are found in the memories created, the lessons learned, and the personal growth achieved along the way. The journey of a treasure hunt teaches patience, resilience, and problem-solving—skills that are invaluable in every aspect of life.

For some, the treasure hunt becomes a metaphor for larger pursuits: finding purpose, achieving dreams, or reconnecting with passions. The process of searching helps uncover treasures not buried in the ground but hidden within ourselves.

The Rise of Modern Treasure Hunting

Treasure hunting is no longer confined to myths and stories. In today's world, people from all walks of life are engaging in hunts for modern-day riches.

- Some search for antiques and collectibles in thrift stores and estate sales.

- Others delve into the digital realm, seeking unclaimed Bitcoin wallets or other cryptocurrency windfalls.

- Adventurers explore shipwrecks, caves, and forgotten trails in pursuit of lost artifacts.

The democratization of tools like GPS, drones, and metal detectors has made treasure hunting accessible to more people than ever before. Social media and online forums allow enthusiasts to share tips, maps, and stories, creating a global community of seekers united by their love of discovery.

What This Book Offers

This book is more than a guide to treasure hunting; it's an invitation to embark on an adventure. Through these pages, you'll learn:

- **The history and psychology of treasure hunting**: What drives people to dedicate their lives to the search?

- **Practical tips and strategies**: How to decode maps, use tools, and navigate challenges.

- **Fascinating stories of real-life discoveries**: From ancient artifacts to modern riches.

- **Lessons for personal growth**: How the journey can transform your perspective on wealth, success, and purpose.

Whether you're seeking material riches or metaphorical treasures, this book provides the tools, knowledge, and inspiration to begin your hunt. You'll uncover the keys to finding hidden treasures—both in the world and within yourself.

The Journey Begins

As we dive into this journey together, remember that the treasure you seek may not always be what you expect. The adventure itself often holds the greatest rewards. So, take a deep breath, gather your tools, and prepare for the hunt of a lifetime. The treasures of the world—and the treasures within—are waiting for you to uncover them.

Your journey begins now. Will you answer the call?

<u>Chapter 2: A History of Treasure Hunts</u>

Treasure hunting has captivated human imagination for centuries, offering tales of riches, adventure, and mystery that transcend time and culture. Whether rooted in historical fact or legend, these stories reflect our shared desire for discovery and the allure of the unknown. In this chapter, we'll delve into the rich history of treasure hunts, uncovering some of the most famous tales, their cultural significance, and how they shaped the practice of treasure hunting today.

The Origins of Treasure Hunting

The concept of treasure is as old as civilization itself. Ancient societies buried their wealth for various reasons, ranging from protection to ceremonial practices. For example:

- **Ancient Egyptians**: Pharaohs were buried with immense treasures to ensure a prosperous afterlife. Tombs like King Tutankhamun's are among the most significant archaeological discoveries in history.

- **Viking Hoards**: The Vikings buried their treasures—gold, silver, and jewelry—as offerings to their gods or to safeguard wealth during times of unrest. Many such hoards have been unearthed in Scandinavia and the British Isles.

- **Chinese Dynasties**: Ancient Chinese emperors buried themselves with treasures, including terracotta armies, to display their power and prepare for the afterlife.

These early practices not only protected wealth but also created the foundation for treasure-hunting myths that persist today.

Legends of Lost Treasures

Some of the most famous treasure hunts are tied to myths and legends, often blending historical fact with fantasy. These tales have inspired adventurers for centuries:

1. **El Dorado: The City of Gold**
   In the 16th century, Spanish conquistadors searched tirelessly for El Dorado, a mythical city rumored to be filled with gold. While the city was never found, the legend highlighted the Europeans' insatiable hunger for wealth and spurred exploration of South America's vast jungles and rivers.

2. **The Knights Templar and the Holy Grail**

The Knights Templar, a medieval Christian military order, were believed to have hidden vast treasures, including the Holy Grail and sacred relics. Over centuries, treasure hunters have scoured Europe and the Middle East in search of these fabled artifacts, intertwining history with spiritual intrigue.

3. **Blackbeard's Hidden Gold**

The notorious pirate Blackbeard was said to have buried his loot along the American East Coast. While no definitive treasure has been found, his story fuels the romantic image of pirates and their legendary hidden riches.

4. **The Lost Dutchman's Mine**

Deep in Arizona's Superstition Mountains lies a tale of gold beyond imagination. The Lost Dutchman's Mine has lured treasure seekers for over a century, despite its exact location being shrouded in mystery.

Real-Life Treasures and Discoveries

Not all treasure tales are myths. History is replete with stories of real treasures discovered after being lost for centuries.

1. **The Tomb of King Tutankhamun**

   In 1922, British archaeologist Howard Carter unearthed the tomb of the young Egyptian pharaoh Tutankhamun. The discovery included a wealth of gold artifacts, jewelry, and treasures that had been hidden for over 3,000 years.

2. **The San Jose Galleon**

   In 1708, the Spanish galleon San Jose sank off the coast of Colombia, laden with gold, silver, and emeralds from the Americas. Rediscovered in 2015, its treasure is valued at billions of dollars, making it one of the most significant underwater finds.

3. **Forrest Fenn's Treasure**

   In 2010, art dealer Forrest Fenn hid a chest containing gold, jewels, and rare artifacts in the Rocky Mountains. He published a cryptic poem as a clue to its location, sparking a decade-long hunt that ended in 2020 when the treasure was finally found.

The Evolution of Treasure Hunting

Treasure hunting has transformed over time, influenced by advancements in technology and shifts in societal values.

1. **Traditional   Methods**

   Early treasure hunters relied on rudimentary tools, folklore, and maps often passed down through generations. These maps, marked with enigmatic symbols or phrases, were as much riddles as they were guides.

2. **Modern   Tools   and   Techniques**

   Today, treasure hunters use sophisticated tools such as:

   - **Metal Detectors**: To locate buried metals with precision.

   - **GPS Technology**: For mapping and navigation in remote locations.

   - **Drones**: To survey difficult terrains from above.

   - **Sonar and Diving Equipment**: For underwater exploration.

3. **Community**   **Collaboration**

Online forums, social media, and global treasure-hunting communities allow enthusiasts to share tips, solve puzzles collectively, and inspire new generations of seekers.

The Impact of Treasure Hunting on Society

Treasure hunts have left a lasting legacy, influencing not only individuals but entire cultures and economies.

- **Cultural Significance**: Treasures, whether real or mythical, are often tied to national identities. The discovery of historical artifacts can redefine a country's history and pride.

- **Economic Influence**: Historical hunts for gold and silver drove colonization and global trade. Today, discoveries like shipwrecks and archaeological sites bring tourism and academic interest to their locations.

- **Personal Transformation**: Beyond monetary rewards, treasure hunting offers a journey of self-discovery, teaching resilience, patience, and creativity.

Lessons from History

The history of treasure hunts reminds us that the journey often holds as much value as the prize. For every treasure found, countless remain hidden, sparking curiosity and inspiring the next generation of seekers. Whether motivated by wealth, adventure, or historical fascination, treasure hunters have always shared a common bond: the relentless pursuit of the extraordinary.

As you read on, let these stories from history guide your own journey. The treasures of the past are not just about gold or jewels—they are lessons in courage, perseverance, and the thrill of exploration.

Chapter 3: The Treasures Within: What's Hidden and Why It Matters

Every treasure hunt begins with a simple yet powerful question: What lies hidden? In the case of *There's Treasure Inside*, the treasures range from physical objects of immense value to the intangible rewards of discovery. This chapter explores the nature of the treasures Jon Collins-Black has hidden across America, why they were chosen, and how each item holds significance far beyond its monetary worth.

A Kaleidoscope of Treasures

The treasures hidden by Jon Collins-Black are as diverse as the people who seek them. Each item was carefully selected to appeal to a wide array of interests, ensuring that this hunt is not just about wealth but also about connecting with history, art, and culture.

1. **Rare and Valuable Objects**

- **Gold and Precious Metals**: Gold bars, coins, and nuggets are timeless treasures, universally recognized for their intrinsic value and symbolism of wealth.

- **Gems and Jewelry**: Rare gemstones such as sapphires, emeralds, and diamonds bring beauty and allure, each carrying a story of its formation over millions of years.

- **Antiquities and Artifacts**: Items from ancient civilizations remind us of the rich tapestry of human history. Examples include Roman coins, Egyptian amulets, and Native American relics.

2. Historical Memorabilia

- **Artifacts with Famous Origins**: Items owned or created by iconic figures, such as a sketch by Pablo Picasso or a letter signed by George Washington, hold immense historical significance.

- **Sports and Pop Culture Memorabilia**: Rare baseball cards, autographed jerseys, and vintage Pokémon cards cater to enthusiasts who value nostalgia and fandom.

3. **Modern-Day Fortunes**

   ○ **Cryptocurrency**: Bitcoin wallets included in the treasure add a futuristic twist, bridging the gap between traditional and contemporary wealth.

The Stories Behind the Treasures

Every treasure hidden by Collins-Black carries a story that adds depth to its value. These narratives transform objects from mere collectibles into pieces of a larger legacy.

1. **The   Picasso   Sketch**
   This sketch, believed to have been a draft for one of Picasso's masterpieces, represents the creative process of one of history's greatest artists. Finding this treasure connects the hunter to the journey of artistic genius.

2. **George   Washington's   Letter**
   A rare letter from the first President of the United States offers a glimpse into the mindset of a founding father. Its value lies not only in its rarity but also in the insight it provides into the birth of a nation.

3. **Shipwreck**   **Artifacts**

   Items salvaged from historic shipwrecks like the Spanish galleons of the 16th century hold stories of exploration, conquest, and tragedy. These treasures remind us of humanity's enduring spirit of adventure.

4. **Pieces of the Forrest Fenn Treasure**

   By including elements from the now-famous Fenn treasure, Collins-Black links his hunt to a modern legend, creating continuity and passing the torch to a new generation of treasure hunters.

Why These Treasures Matter

The treasures hidden in this hunt go beyond monetary value. They were chosen to inspire, educate, and connect people to the broader human experience.

1. **Inspiration**

   These treasures are a call to action, encouraging seekers to embrace curiosity, take risks, and step out of their comfort zones. The idea of uncovering something extraordinary fuels hope and ambition.

2. Education

Many treasures in this hunt are tied to historical events, famous figures, or cultural movements. By seeking these items, participants learn about art, history, and innovation, enriching their understanding of the world.

3. Connection

The diversity of the treasures reflects the diversity of humanity. Each item resonates differently with individuals, fostering a sense of shared purpose among participants and a connection to those who came before us.

The Intangible Treasures

While the physical treasures in this hunt are undeniably exciting, the true rewards often lie in the journey itself.

1. Personal   Growth

The act of hunting for treasure—solving puzzles, navigating challenges, and persevering through setbacks—builds resilience, critical thinking, and creativity. These skills are invaluable in all areas of life.

2. **Relationships**

Many treasure hunters work in teams, forming bonds through shared experiences. The hunt fosters collaboration and camaraderie, creating memories that outlast the pursuit.

3. **The   Thrill   of   Discovery**

The moment of uncovering a hidden treasure is one of pure joy and triumph. It's not just about the object but the realization of a dream and the culmination of effort and determination.

The Greater Purpose of the Hunt

Jon Collins-Black designed this treasure hunt with a purpose beyond wealth. By scattering treasures across America, he invites participants to explore the nation's landscapes, history, and culture. The hunt encourages people to:

- **Rediscover Forgotten Places**: Many treasures are hidden in locations with historical or ecological significance, drawing attention to areas that deserve preservation and appreciation.

- **Celebrate Diversity**: The varied nature of the treasures reflects the diversity of human achievement, reminding seekers of the many ways people have contributed to the world.

- **Embrace Adventure**: In an age of technology and convenience, this hunt brings back the thrill of real-world exploration.

What Awaits You

The treasures within this hunt are more than material riches. They are keys to unlocking personal growth, shared experiences, and a deeper connection to history and humanity.

As you embark on this journey, remember that every step is part of the reward. The treasures you uncover may shine brightly in your hands, but the memories, lessons, and relationships you gain along the way will shine even brighter in your heart.

The next chapter will guide you through the tools, strategies, and mindset needed to embark on this extraordinary adventure. Prepare to chart your course and take the first steps toward uncovering the treasures within.

Chapter 4: The Map to Riches: Clues, Riddles, and the Art of Discovery

In the world of treasure hunting, the journey to discovery is often as exhilarating as the treasure itself. The hunt for Jon Collins-Black's hidden treasures is no different. With carefully designed clues, cryptic riddles, and intricate maps, this chapter explores the tools that lead seekers to unimaginable riches. You'll learn how to interpret the hints, approach the riddles, and adopt a strategic mindset for success.

The Treasure Map: An Overview

Jon Collins-Black's treasure hunt doesn't rely on a single physical map. Instead, it's a collection of clues woven into the pages of *There's Treasure Inside*. Each clue, whether in the form of a riddle, a historical reference, or a cryptographic challenge, serves as a breadcrumb, leading the seeker closer to a hidden prize.

1. **Clues Embedded in the Book**

- Passages in the text include subtle hints, such as geographic coordinates, historical markers, or word puzzles.

- The artwork and typography may hold visual clues. A seemingly decorative border could reveal a pattern that points to a treasure's location.

2. Digital Extensions

- QR codes within the book direct readers to exclusive online content, including additional clues, interactive maps, and forums for collaboration.

- Social media accounts and email updates from Collins-Black occasionally drop bonus hints.

3. Physical Maps and Locations

- Some treasures are tied to famous landmarks, national parks, or historically significant sites. The book includes detailed descriptions of these places, encouraging seekers to connect with the locations on a deeper level.

Deciphering the Clues

To uncover the treasures, seekers must become adept at decoding a variety of clue types. Here's how to approach them:

1. **Cryptic Riddles**

   o **Example**: "Where shadows fall at noon, the past stands tall; beneath the earth lies fortune's call."

   o **Interpretation**: The riddle might refer to an ancient monument or a location associated with shadows, such as a sundial.

   o **Strategy**: Break the riddle into parts, identify keywords, and research their historical or cultural significance.

2. **Numeric Codes**

   o Some clues may involve sequences of numbers, like GPS coordinates or cryptographic ciphers.

   o Learn to recognize common patterns, such as Morse code, Caesar ciphers, or binary conversions.

3. **Historical References**

- Many clues allude to historical events, figures, or artifacts. For instance, a reference to the Boston Tea Party might point to a treasure hidden near Boston Harbor.

- Research the historical context of the clue to find connections to potential locations.

4. **Visual Hints**

- Analyze illustrations, photographs, or diagrams in the book. These images may contain hidden symbols, letters, or landmarks that provide valuable guidance.

- Pay attention to details like unusual shapes, colors, or placements.

The Role of Research and Technology

Modern treasure hunting often requires a combination of traditional research skills and cutting-edge technology.

1. **Online Research**

- Use search engines, databases, and archives to investigate historical references or geographical hints.

- Treasure-hunting forums and online communities can offer collaborative insights.

2. Geographic Tools

- Applications like Google Earth allow seekers to explore potential locations remotely.

- Topographic maps, available online or in bookstores, help identify physical features mentioned in the clues.

3. Specialized Equipment

- Metal detectors, compasses, and GPS devices can assist when searching in the field.

- For underwater or remote searches, drones and sonar equipment may be necessary.

The Importance of Strategy

Success in treasure hunting requires more than just solving clues—it demands a clear strategy and organized approach.

1. Planning Your Hunt

- Choose a specific treasure to focus on rather than pursuing all at once.

- Create a timeline and checklist to track your progress.

2. **Collaborating with Others**

- Team up with friends or fellow seekers to pool resources and insights.

- Sharing perspectives can help solve complex clues faster.

3. **Staying Persistent**

- Not every lead will result in a discovery. Learn to treat setbacks as learning experiences and keep moving forward.

Safety and Ethical Considerations

Treasure hunting can be thrilling but also comes with responsibilities.

1. **Safety First**

- Always prepare for the physical demands of your search. Carry essentials such as water, first-aid kits, and proper clothing for the environment.

- Inform someone about your plans, especially if searching in remote or challenging locations.

2. Respect for Protected Sites

- Some treasures may be hidden near historical landmarks or protected lands. Ensure your search complies with local laws and regulations.

- Avoid causing damage to the environment or disturbing wildlife.

3. Ethical Treasure Hunting

- If you uncover historically significant artifacts, consider reporting them to appropriate authorities or museums.

- Share your discoveries responsibly, respecting the heritage and value of the items you find.

The Joy of Discovery

The thrill of deciphering clues and piecing together the puzzle is one of the most rewarding aspects of the hunt. Each solved riddle, uncovered location, and discovered treasure becomes part of your personal journey.

As you engage with the map of clues in *There's Treasure Inside*, remember that the hunt is not just about material wealth. It's an opportunity to explore new places, connect with history, and embrace the spirit of adventure.

In the next chapter, we'll dive deeper into the locations where treasures may be hidden and the role these settings play in shaping the overall experience of the hunt. Prepare to journey through America's landscapes, from bustling cities to serene wilderness, as you continue your quest for riches.

Chapter 5: The Landscape of Discovery: Where Treasures Lie

The United States, with its vast expanse and rich tapestry of history, culture, and geography, is the ultimate treasure map. Jon Collins-Black carefully selected the hiding places for his treasures, ensuring they are not only challenging to find but also meaningful in their context. In this chapter, we delve into the diverse landscapes where the treasures lie, exploring the significance of these locations and the stories they tell.

The Philosophy Behind the Locations

Jon Collins-Black didn't hide his treasures randomly. Each location was chosen with intent, reflecting themes of history, beauty, and adventure. These sites:

- **Inspire Exploration**: Encouraging hunters to venture into new environments and rediscover forgotten places.

- **Celebrate Heritage**: Many treasures are linked to historical events, figures, or eras, tying their value to a broader cultural narrative.

- **Highlight Diversity**: The chosen locations span urban centers, natural wonders, and everything in between, showcasing the variety and richness of the United States.

Urban Landscapes: Treasures in the Heart of the City

Cities are hubs of human history and innovation, making them perfect places to hide treasures with cultural or historical significance.

1. **Historic Landmarks**

   - Treasures might be hidden near iconic structures like the Statue of Liberty, the Liberty Bell, or the Golden Gate Bridge. These locations symbolize freedom, innovation, and perseverance.

   - Example: A clue might lead to a time capsule buried in Central Park, connecting seekers to a specific moment in the city's vibrant history.

2. **Cultural Centers**

- Museums, libraries, and theaters often house treasures of knowledge and creativity. Some hidden items may be placed near such institutions to honor the arts and sciences.
- Example: A riddle referencing "pages that never sleep" could guide hunters to the New York Public Library.

3. **Hidden Gems in the Urban Jungle**

- Treasures could also be located in lesser-known areas, such as historic neighborhoods or overlooked parks, encouraging seekers to explore the lesser-known facets of a city.

Natural Wonders: Treasures in the Wild

The natural world has always been a source of inspiration and mystery. Many treasures are hidden in America's breathtaking landscapes, urging seekers to connect with the environment.

1. **National Parks and Forests**

- Iconic parks like Yellowstone, Yosemite, and the Grand Canyon are prime locations for treasures that celebrate nature's grandeur.

- Example: A golden nugget might be hidden near Old Faithful, accompanied by a clue about "the timeless pulse of the earth."

2. Mountain Ranges

- The Rockies, Appalachians, and Sierra Nevada offer dramatic terrains for adventurous seekers. Treasures here are likely to test both physical endurance and problem-solving skills.

- Example: A cryptic message about "ascending to the eagle's perch" could lead hunters to a high-altitude location with panoramic views.

3. Rivers and Lakes

- Waterways like the Mississippi River or Lake Tahoe hold historical and ecological significance. Treasures hidden near these locations remind seekers of their importance to America's development.

- Example: A treasure buried near the banks of the Missouri River might come with a riddle referencing Lewis and Clark's expedition.

Cultural and Historical Hotspots

Some treasures are placed in locations that highlight pivotal moments in American history or the achievements of remarkable individuals.

1. **Revolutionary War Sites**

   - Places like Valley Forge and Boston Harbor connect seekers to the birth of American independence.

   - Example: A treasure clue referencing "tea spilled in rebellion" could point to a hiding spot in Boston.

2. **Civil Rights Movement Landmarks**

   - Locations tied to the fight for equality, such as Selma or the Martin Luther King Jr. Memorial, serve as poignant reminders of progress and struggle.

- Example: A treasure might be hidden in Montgomery, Alabama, with a clue celebrating "the steps that changed a nation."

3. **Pioneering Achievements**

- Locations tied to technological or cultural breakthroughs, such as the Wright Brothers' flight site in Kitty Hawk or Silicon Valley, honor the spirit of innovation.

Remote and Unexpected Locations

While some treasures are hidden in well-known areas, others lie in remote or surprising locations, waiting for the most adventurous hunters.

1. **Deserts and Badlands**

- The arid beauty of places like Death Valley or the Badlands National Park presents both a challenge and a reward for those willing to brave the elements.

- Example: A treasure buried in the shadow of an ancient petrified tree might come with a clue about "the bones of giants."

2. Small Towns and Forgotten Places

- Some treasures are located in towns off the beaten path, preserving their charm and inviting seekers to discover hidden stories.

- Example: A treasure in a quiet Midwest town might celebrate the legacy of a local hero or inventor.

3. Coastal Wonders

- Beaches, cliffs, and islands along America's coastlines offer serene yet challenging environments for treasure hunting.

- Example: A chest hidden in a sea cave on the Oregon coast might include a clue referencing "the whispers of the tide."

The Challenges of the Landscape

Hunting for treasures across such a diverse array of locations comes with unique challenges, including:

- **Physical Demands**: Some terrains require strength, stamina, or special equipment to navigate.

- **Weather and Seasons**: Certain locations may be accessible only during specific times of the year, adding an element of timing to the hunt.

- **Permits and Permissions**: National parks and historical sites may have rules governing excavation or exploration, necessitating careful planning.

Environmental and Cultural Responsibility

Jon Collins-Black designed the hunt to inspire appreciation for America's landscapes and history, not to harm or exploit them. Treasure hunters are encouraged to:

- **Respect the Environment**: Avoid damaging natural habitats or disturbing wildlife while searching.

- **Preserve Historical Integrity**: Follow all local regulations and respect the cultural significance of the sites you visit.

- **Leave No Trace**: Ensure your search leaves the environment as pristine as you found it.

A Journey Through America's Soul

The treasures hidden across America's cities, wilderness, and historical landmarks are not just objects of value—they're an invitation to explore the essence of the nation. Each location tells a story, offers a lesson, and inspires a sense of wonder.

As you continue your quest, remember that the treasures you seek are as much about the journey as they are about the discovery. In the next chapter, we'll discuss the skills and tools you need to tackle the challenges of treasure hunting effectively, ensuring you're ready for the adventure that lies ahead.

Chapter 6: Tools of the Trade: Essential Skills and Gear for Treasure Hunters

Embarking on a treasure hunt is not just about decoding clues or exploring intriguing locations. Success often depends on preparation, both in terms of the skills you bring and the tools you carry. In this chapter, we'll delve into the essential skills and equipment every treasure hunter needs, highlighting practical tips and techniques to enhance your chances of uncovering hidden riches.

The Skills Every Treasure Hunter Needs

While a sense of adventure is the foundation of any treasure hunt, honing specific skills can make the difference between success and failure.

1. Problem-Solving and Analytical Thinking

- **Why It Matters**: Treasure hunting often involves deciphering riddles, solving puzzles, and interpreting complex clues.

- **How to Develop It**:

  - Practice with brainteasers, crossword puzzles, and logic games to sharpen your cognitive abilities.

  - Study historical ciphers, codes, and symbols to prepare for cryptographic challenges.

  - Approach each clue methodically, breaking it into smaller, manageable components.

---

2. Geography and Map Reading

- **Why It Matters**: Many treasures are hidden in specific geographic locations, often referenced through maps or GPS coordinates.

- **How to Develop It**:

  - Learn to read topographic maps, focusing on contours, elevations, and landmarks.

  - Practice using a compass and understanding cardinal directions.

  - Familiarize yourself with GPS tools and applications like Google Earth or offline mapping software.

3. Research and Historical Knowledge

- **Why It Matters**: Clues often reference historical events, figures, or artifacts, requiring background knowledge to interpret.

- **How to Develop It**:

  o Dive into books, documentaries, and online resources about American history, geography, and culture.

  o Join forums or online communities where treasure hunters discuss and analyze clues.

  o Explore archives, libraries, and databases to uncover hidden connections.

4. Outdoor Survival Skills

- **Why It Matters**: Some treasures are hidden in remote or rugged locations, where navigating the environment safely is crucial.

- **How to Develop It**:

- Learn basic survival skills, including building a shelter, starting a fire, and sourcing clean water.

- Take a first-aid course to handle minor injuries during your search.

- Practice hiking, climbing, or kayaking if the terrain requires specialized techniques.

5. Attention to Detail

- **Why It Matters**: Small details in clues or locations can lead to significant discoveries.

- **How to Develop It**:

  - Cultivate mindfulness and observation skills by studying your surroundings during practice searches.

  - Revisit clues or locations multiple times, as a fresh perspective can reveal overlooked details.

The Essential Gear for Treasure Hunting

Equipping yourself with the right tools can enhance your efficiency and safety while treasure hunting. Here's a comprehensive list:

1. Navigation Tools

- **Maps and Compass**: Always carry physical maps and a reliable compass as backups to electronic devices.

- **GPS Devices**: A handheld GPS unit or smartphone with offline maps can pinpoint precise locations.

2. Exploration Equipment

- **Metal Detector**: Useful for locating buried treasures like coins, relics, or artifacts.

- **Digging Tools**: Carry a sturdy shovel, trowel, or digging knife for excavating treasures.

- **Magnifying Glass**: Helps inspect small details in clues or artifacts.

3. Safety Gear

- **First-Aid Kit**: Include bandages, antiseptic wipes, and any personal medications.

- **Protective Clothing**: Wear sturdy boots, gloves, and weather-appropriate attire.

- **Flashlight or Headlamp**: Ensure visibility in caves, tunnels, or during nighttime searches.

---

4. Technology and Gadgets

- **Camera or Smartphone**: Document your journey and capture clues for later analysis.

- **Portable Charger**: Keep your electronic devices powered in remote areas.

- **Drones**: Use drones for aerial reconnaissance in hard-to-reach locations.

---

5. Research and Documentation Tools

- **Notebook and Pen**: Jot down observations, decoded clues, or potential leads.

- **Reference Materials**: Carry printouts or guides related to the clues or historical references you're investigating.

Techniques for Efficient Treasure Hunting

Having the right skills and gear is only half the equation. Applying effective techniques will maximize your chances of success.

---

1. Clue Organization

- **How to Do It**:

  - Create a spreadsheet or journal to log all discovered clues and their possible interpretations.

  - Group similar clues together, as they may relate to the same treasure.

---

2. Field Planning

- **How to Do It**:

  - Before heading out, study the terrain and identify potential obstacles or hazards.

  - Plan your route carefully, marking key waypoints on a map.

  - Always have a backup plan in case weather or other factors disrupt your search.

---

3. Team Collaboration

- **How to Do It**:

  - Work with a team to pool knowledge and resources.

  - Assign roles based on individual strengths, such as deciphering clues, navigating, or excavation.

---

4. Adaptability and Patience

- **How to Do It**:

- Stay flexible and open-minded. A clue may have multiple interpretations, and persistence often pays off.

- Celebrate small victories, like solving part of a riddle or reaching a challenging location, to maintain morale.

Real-World Examples of Tools and Techniques in Action

To illustrate these principles, consider the case of treasure hunter Mark Daniels, who discovered a hidden artifact in the Colorado Rockies.

- **Clue Decoding**: He used his knowledge of local history to identify a reference to an abandoned mining town.

- **Navigation**: Equipped with a GPS unit and a detailed topographic map, he pinpointed the treasure's location.

- **Persistence**: Despite several failed attempts, his determination and adaptability ultimately led to success.

Building Your Treasure Hunter's Toolkit

As you prepare for your hunt, remember that your tools and skills are an extension of your ingenuity and passion.

- Start small, practicing with local searches or puzzles.

- Gradually invest in specialized equipment as your experience grows.

- Join treasure-hunting communities to exchange tips and expand your network.

Chapter 7: The Psychology of the Hunt: What Drives Treasure Seekers?

Treasure hunting is more than a quest for material wealth. It taps into deeply ingrained human instincts and psychological motivations. In this chapter, we explore the psychological underpinnings of treasure hunting, examining what drives people to dedicate their time, energy, and resources to this pursuit. Whether it's the thrill of the unknown, the allure of riches, or the desire for legacy, understanding these motivations can provide invaluable insight into your own treasure-hunting journey.

The Thrill of Discovery

At the heart of every treasure hunt is the thrill of discovery. This primal emotion is tied to our evolutionary history as hunters and gatherers.

1. The Dopamine Effect

- **How It Works**:

- Dopamine, the brain's reward chemical, surges during activities associated with potential rewards, such as solving puzzles or uncovering clues.

- This creates a feedback loop: each small success in the hunt encourages further effort.

- **Why It Matters**:

  - Understanding the brain's reward system can help you stay motivated, even during setbacks.

---

2. The Mystery Factor

- **The Science**:

  - Humans are naturally curious, and mysteries stimulate brain activity associated with problem-solving and imagination.

- **The Treasure Hunting Context**:

  - Each clue or artifact represents a piece of the puzzle, driving hunters to seek closure and answers.

The Allure of Wealth and Status

While the treasure itself is often a powerful motivator, its perceived value extends beyond material wealth.

---

1. Wealth as a Symbol

- **Cultural Significance**:
  - Gold, gems, and other valuables have symbolized power, success, and security throughout history.

- **The Modern Context**:
  - For some, the pursuit of treasure represents the dream of financial freedom or the opportunity to rewrite their life story.

2. Social Recognition

- **The Appeal of Fame**:
  - Discovering a hidden treasure often garners media attention and recognition, elevating the finder to a position of prestige.

- **Legacy Building**:

- Many treasure hunters seek to leave a mark on history, immortalizing their achievements for future generations.

The Quest for Adventure

Treasure hunting appeals to the adventurer within, offering an escape from the monotony of everyday life.

---

1. Exploration and Freedom

- **The Psychological Appeal**:

  - The act of venturing into uncharted territories satisfies our innate desire for exploration and freedom.

- **Real-Life Stories**:

  - Countless hunters describe the journey itself as more rewarding than the actual treasure, highlighting the transformative power of adventure.

2. Facing Challenges

- **The Role of Risk**:
  - Overcoming obstacles—be it decoding complex riddles, enduring harsh weather, or navigating rugged terrain—creates a sense of accomplishment and builds resilience.

The Power of Stories

Human beings are storytellers at heart, and treasure hunting allows us to create and live out our own narratives.

---

1. Living a Legend

- **Connection to History**:
  - Many treasure hunters are drawn to the idea of stepping into the shoes of historical figures or unraveling age-old mysteries.

- **The Impact**:
  - This connection to the past adds depth and meaning to the search, making each discovery feel like a chapter in a larger story.

2. Crafting a Personal Saga

- **Your Story**:

  - As you hunt for treasure, you're creating a story that's uniquely yours—one filled with challenges, triumphs, and unforgettable moments.

The Psychological Pitfalls of Treasure Hunting

While the pursuit of treasure can be exhilarating, it also comes with emotional risks and challenges. Awareness of these pitfalls can help you navigate them effectively.

---

1. Obsession

- **The Danger**:

  - The hunt can become all-consuming, leading some to neglect relationships, work, or personal well-being.

- **How to Avoid It**:

  - Set clear boundaries for your treasure-hunting activities and maintain balance in your life.

2. Disappointment

- **The Reality**:
  - Not every search ends in success, and repeated setbacks can take an emotional toll.

- **Coping Strategies**:
  - Focus on the journey rather than the outcome, and view each search as an opportunity to learn and grow.

3. Competition and Conflict

- **The Challenge**:
  - Competing with other treasure hunters can create tension or lead to disputes over discoveries.

- **How to Handle It**:
  - Approach the hunt with a spirit of collaboration and goodwill, valuing camaraderie over competition.

Psychological Growth Through Treasure Hunting

Despite its challenges, treasure hunting offers immense potential for personal growth and transformation.

1. Building Resilience

- **How It Happens:**

  - Facing and overcoming obstacles strengthens your ability to handle adversity in all areas of life.

2. Fostering Creativity

- **Why It Matters:**

  - The process of solving clues and thinking outside the box enhances creative problem-solving skills.

3. Deepening Connections

- **The Social Aspect:**

  - Many hunters form lifelong friendships or deepen existing relationships through shared adventures.

Chapter 8: The Legends and Myths Behind America's Hidden Treasures

Throughout history, hidden treasures have captivated the human imagination, sparking adventures, inspiring legends, and creating a rich tapestry of stories that have been passed down through generations. These treasures are often shrouded in mystery, with rumors, folklore, and myths surrounding them. In this chapter, we will explore some of America's most famous hidden treasures—stories that continue to inspire treasure hunters and adventurers to this day. By delving into these legends, we will examine the historical, cultural, and psychological reasons why these myths endure.

1. The Lost Confederate Treasure

One of the most enduring and tantalizing treasure myths in American history revolves around the Lost Confederate Treasure.

The Legend

- **The Backstory**: During the closing days of the Civil War, the Confederacy was in disarray, and it's believed that Confederate officials, including President Jefferson Davis, hid a substantial amount of gold, silver, and other valuable items to keep them out of Union hands. The treasure was allegedly hidden somewhere in the Southern states, possibly in Georgia, Alabama, or even as far west as Texas.

- **Key Elements**:

  - The treasure's value is estimated to be in the millions of dollars, including gold bullion, coins, and Confederate bonds.

  - Various clues have surfaced over the years, leading treasure hunters to sift through old documents and maps, searching for hints of the treasure's location.

Why It Endures

- **Cultural and Historical Significance**: The Lost Confederate Treasure represents the last hope of the Confederacy during a time of loss and defeat. It's a symbol of resistance and rebellion, woven into the fabric of the South's identity.

- **Psychological Appeal**: The allure of finding the treasure of the "losing side" of the Civil War taps into a sense of uncovering hidden truths and restoring the lost honor of a defeated people.

---

2. The Oak Island Mystery

Oak Island, located off the coast of Nova Scotia, is not technically in the United States, but it has close ties to American treasure hunters due to its proximity and the historical involvement of early American explorers.

The Legend

- **The Backstory**: In 1795, a young boy named Daniel McGinnis discovered a mysterious depression in the ground while exploring Oak Island. Over time, numerous attempts to dig for treasure at the site uncovered layers of wood, stone, and other strange markers, suggesting that something valuable was buried deep beneath the surface.

- **Key Elements**:

- Theories about the treasure range from hidden pirate loot to the lost treasures of the Knights Templar, with some even speculating that the Ark of the Covenant may be buried on the island.

- Despite centuries of excavation, no treasure has been conclusively found, though several intriguing artifacts have surfaced, including coins, stone inscriptions, and parts of what some believe to be a treasure chest.

Why It Endures

- **Mystery and Intrigue**: The Oak Island mystery captivates because it has never been definitively solved. It's a puzzle that continues to tantalize treasure hunters, with each excavation revealing more questions than answers.

- **The Psychological Pull of the Unsolvable**: The idea of a treasure being just out of reach, waiting to be unearthed by the next person, feeds into the allure of human curiosity and the desire for discovery.

3. The Lost Dutchman's Gold Mine

Possibly the most famous treasure legend in the American Southwest, the Lost Dutchman's Gold Mine has lured adventurers into the Arizona desert for more than a century.

The Legend

- **The Backstory**: The story of the Lost Dutchman's Gold Mine dates back to the 1840s, when a German immigrant named Jacob Waltz reportedly discovered a rich vein of gold in the Superstition Mountains east of Phoenix, Arizona. Waltz kept the location of the mine secret, and before his death in 1891, he reportedly gave cryptic clues to a few trusted individuals. Since then, treasure hunters have been searching for the mine, but no one has ever conclusively found it.

- **Key Elements**:
  - The treasure is said to be so vast that it could have enriched the entire region, but it's hidden in a treacherous and remote location in the rugged Superstition Mountains.

- Many who have ventured into the mountains in search of the mine have disappeared, adding an element of danger to the legend.

Why It Endures

- **The Appeal of the Frontier**: The Lost Dutchman's Gold Mine is tied to the myth of the American frontier—untamed land where fortune and danger awaited.

- **The Curse**: The legend is often accompanied by warnings about a "curse" that strikes down those who seek the gold. This curse, combined with the harsh conditions of the Superstition Mountains, heightens the mystique of the treasure.

- **The Challenge of the Search**: The treasure hunt for the Lost Dutchman's Mine is one of endurance and survival. The idea of braving the elements and overcoming danger for the promise of unimaginable wealth speaks to the human need for adventure and overcoming hardship.

4. The Legend of the Santo Niño Treasure

A lesser-known but equally fascinating treasure story is that of the Santo Niño Treasure, which dates back to the Spanish colonial era.

The Legend

- **The Backstory**: During the 16th century, Spanish conquistadors, facing pressure from Native American resistance and rival European powers, buried large amounts of gold, silver, and religious artifacts in the southwestern United States, primarily in what is now New Mexico and Arizona. One of the most intriguing of these treasures is the Santo Niño Treasure, which is rumored to be hidden near the ruins of an old Spanish mission in New Mexico.

- **Key Elements**:
  - The treasure includes gold coins, chalices, and religious relics, possibly hidden by Franciscan priests as they fled from Apache attacks.

- Some believe the treasure is associated with the statue of Santo Niño (the Holy Child), which could be the key to locating the hidden cache.

Why It Endures

- **The Legacy of Spanish Exploration**: The allure of the Santo Niño Treasure lies in its connection to the Spanish exploration and colonization of the American Southwest. The treasure hunt symbolizes both religious devotion and the search for wealth during a tumultuous time in history.

- **Mystical and Religious Undertones**: The legend is imbued with religious imagery, as the treasure is tied to sacred objects and a divine protector. This adds a layer of spiritual significance to the hunt.

---

5. The Forrest Fenn Treasure

The Forrest Fenn Treasure, hidden by art dealer and author Forrest Fenn, has captured the imaginations of thousands of treasure hunters over the last decade.

The Legend

- **The Backstory**: In 2010, Fenn, a wealthy art dealer and adventurer, hid a chest filled with gold, jewels, and other valuable items somewhere in the Rocky Mountains. He released a poem in his autobiography, *The Thrill of the Chase*, which was said to contain clues to the treasure's location. The treasure became the subject of intense search efforts for nearly a decade before it was finally found in 2020.

- **Key Elements**:
  - The chest contained gold nuggets, coins, jewels, and other items worth an estimated $2 million.

  - For nearly a decade, the treasure remained hidden, and the hunt became a widespread phenomenon, with some hunters risking their lives in pursuit of the chest.

Why It Endures

- **Modern-Day Legend**: The Forrest Fenn Treasure is a modern treasure legend, blending contemporary culture with the timeless appeal of buried wealth.

- **The Accessibility of the Hunt**: Unlike many ancient treasures, the Forrest Fenn Treasure was relatively accessible to everyday people, creating a unique and democratic treasure-hunting experience.

- **The Search for Meaning**: For many, the treasure hunt was not just about wealth but about the journey itself—connecting with nature, solving puzzles, and experiencing personal growth.

Chapter 9: The Modern Treasure Hunter: Tools, Strategies, and Techniques

The world of treasure hunting has evolved dramatically in the past few decades. What was once the domain of seasoned explorers armed only with maps and intuition has now become an enterprise enhanced by technology, strategy, and professional-grade tools. In this chapter, we'll dive into the modern techniques, equipment, and strategies that treasure hunters use to find hidden wealth today. Whether you're an amateur hobbyist or a serious seeker, understanding the tools of the trade can help you in your own quest for treasure.

---

1. The Role of Technology in Modern Treasure Hunting

In the past, treasure hunting relied heavily on intuition, folklore, and physical endurance. While these elements still play a role, modern technology has completely revolutionized the treasure hunting game, making it more accessible and precise.

A. Metal Detectors: The Treasure Hunter's Best Friend

- **How They Work**: Metal detectors detect metal objects beneath the earth's surface by sending out electromagnetic fields and measuring the return signals from metallic objects. Modern metal detectors are incredibly sensitive, allowing hunters to pinpoint even small items like coins, jewelry, or artifacts buried in the ground.

- **Key Features**:

  - **Discrimination Settings**: Modern metal detectors can discriminate between different types of metals. This is invaluable for treasure hunters because it allows them to filter out unwanted items like nails or bottle caps.

  - **Depth Indicators**: Many detectors today include depth indicators that can tell you how deep an object might be buried, helping you avoid unnecessary digging.

  - **Advanced Frequency Technology**: High-frequency detectors are great for finding smaller items and deep treasures, while low-frequency models excel at detecting larger and deeper objects.

- **Popular Models**:

  - **Minelab Excalibur II**: Widely regarded as one of the best all-purpose metal detectors, known for its underwater capabilities.

  - **Garrett AT Pro**: A versatile model perfect for both land and water, designed for hunters who need a durable, reliable detector.

B. Ground Penetrating Radar (GPR)

- **How It Works**: Ground Penetrating Radar is one of the most powerful tools used by modern treasure hunters. It sends electromagnetic waves into the ground and detects the reflected signals from underground structures, materials, or objects. GPR can be particularly useful for detecting larger, more hidden caches such as treasure chests, shipwrecks, or abandoned mines.

- **Applications**:

  - Locating large buried objects like treasure chests or shipwrecks.

- Finding hidden structures, such as old tunnels, vaults, or caches of weapons and gold.

- **Benefits**: Unlike metal detectors, GPR can help detect objects made of non-metallic materials, such as wooden chests or even human-made cavities.

- **Challenges**: GPR is expensive and requires a skilled operator to interpret the data, but when used effectively, it can yield incredible results.

C. Drones and Aerial Mapping

- **How They Work**: Drones equipped with high-resolution cameras and GPS technology are increasingly being used in treasure hunting. Drones can capture aerial views of hard-to-reach locations, helping treasure hunters identify patterns in the landscape that may indicate buried or hidden objects.

- **Applications**:
  - Aerial surveys of large areas, particularly remote or difficult-to-access locations.

- High-resolution imagery of archaeological sites or regions with suspected treasure deposits.

- **Benefits**: Drones can cover large areas quickly and efficiently, significantly reducing the time spent on-site.

---

2. Using Maps, Clues, and Research to Locate Treasures

While modern technology is an invaluable tool, no treasure hunt is ever completely reliant on machines. The most successful treasure hunters combine technology with traditional methods—research, map analysis, and a sharp eye for clues.

A. Historical Maps and Documents

- **How They Help**: Maps from the past can offer invaluable insight into where treasures might be hidden. Whether they are old pirate maps, military documents, or records of historical events, these resources often contain the key to a hidden treasure. Maps that document old forts, shipwrecks, battle sites, and Native American settlements are prime candidates for treasure hunters to explore.

- **Where to Find Them**:

  - Local historical societies and libraries often have collections of old maps.

  - Archives and government buildings hold maps from significant historical periods (such as the Civil War).

  - Many rare maps are now digitized and available online through university libraries and private collectors.

B. Reading the Land: Geocaching and Environmental Cues

- **How It Works**: Some treasure hunters rely on environmental cues—natural landmarks and geological features that might indicate where hidden treasures are buried. Rivers, mountains, and rock formations have always served as guideposts in treasure lore. Geocaching, the practice of hiding and finding objects using GPS coordinates, often gives hunters clues about the potential location of hidden artifacts.

- **What to Look For**:

    o Unique rock formations, caves, or ravines.

    o Ancient trees or plants that mark historical events or settlements.

    o Animal tracks, water sources, or other natural signs that have been historically tied to treasure hiding practices.

---

3. Strategies for Success: The Mental and Tactical Edge

Successful treasure hunting isn't just about the right tools—it's about applying them strategically. Experienced treasure hunters know that careful planning and a methodical approach are just as important as the right equipment.

A. Creating a Treasure Hunting Plan

- **Strategic Site Selection**: Before embarking on any hunt, determine your area of focus. Research whether there have been historical discoveries or other treasure hunts in the area, and gather as much information as possible about the location.

- **Mapping Out the Search**: Divide the land into sections and map out each section for focused searches. This allows you to cover a large area efficiently and avoid overlooking hidden objects.

- **Weather Considerations**: Certain times of the year may be more advantageous for treasure hunting. For example, after a heavy rain, the ground may be softer and easier to dig, and the landscape may reveal more clues.

B. Using Clue Analysis and Problem-Solving

- **The Detective's Mindset**: Treasure hunting is a lot like solving a mystery. Each clue you find is a piece of a larger puzzle. Combining historical knowledge with clues from maps, weather, and local legends allows hunters to see patterns that others might miss.

- **Critical Thinking**: Successful treasure hunters need to ask the right questions: Why was this object buried here? What historical events happened in this area? What physical features can guide you to the treasure?

C. Persistence and Patience

- **The Power of Perseverance**: Finding treasure rarely happens on the first try. Most successful treasure hunters fail dozens, if not hundreds, of times before discovering something significant. The key is to stay motivated, follow through, and learn from past mistakes.

- **Dealing with Setbacks**: Treasure hunting can be physically demanding, mentally draining, and emotionally taxing. The treasure itself might be elusive, but the experience of the hunt—the process, the adventure, and the lessons learned—are often just as rewarding.

---

4. Treasure Hunting Ethics and Legal Considerations

It's essential for treasure hunters to understand the ethical and legal aspects of their pursuit. Depending on where you are searching, laws governing the discovery of treasures vary widely. In some regions, items found on private land are legally considered the property of the landowner. However, anything discovered on public lands or in water may be subject to laws protecting cultural heritage.

A. Legal Framework

- **Private Land**: Always obtain permission from the landowner before beginning any hunt on private property. Failing to do so may result in legal consequences, including trespassing charges.

- **Public Land**: Federal and state lands often have strict rules regarding what can be removed from public property. Many public lands are protected as national parks or cultural sites, and it is illegal to remove artifacts from these locations without express permission.

- **Metal Detecting Laws**: Always check local laws regarding metal detecting. Some areas may require permits, while others may prohibit the use of metal detectors altogether.

B. Ethical Considerations

- **Respect for History**: It's important to consider the historical and cultural significance of the treasures you find. Many of the artifacts hunters uncover can provide invaluable information about past civilizations, lost cultures, or significant events in history. It's crucial to approach treasure hunting with a sense of respect and responsibility, ensuring that any discovery contributes to the preservation of history.

- **Sustainable Practices**: Avoid damaging the environment during your treasure hunt. Using the right equipment and techniques can help preserve the land and avoid harming wildlife or ecosystems.

Chapter 10: The Treasure You Can't See: The Real Riches of the Journey

While the allure of finding hidden treasure—gold, rare gems, antiquities—forms the foundation of many treasure hunts, there is a deeper, more profound treasure that comes from the journey itself. This chapter explores the intangible riches found during your pursuit of material wealth: the personal growth, connections with others, historical revelations, and the life-changing experiences that can redefine what treasure truly means. For some, the greatest treasures lie not in what's discovered, but in who you become along the way.

---

1. Personal Growth: Lessons from the Hunt

A treasure hunt is rarely straightforward. It's a journey filled with uncertainty, challenges, and unexpected twists. Throughout this journey, you will encounter obstacles—both physical and mental—that require patience, resilience, and creativity. These are the moments where you'll experience the greatest personal growth.

A. Patience and Persistence: The Virtues of the Treasure Hunter

- **Endurance Through Failure**: Rarely do treasure hunters strike gold on their first try. The search is long, often filled with disappointments and false leads. But it's in these moments that you'll learn the most about perseverance. Each failed attempt is not a failure, but a learning experience—an opportunity to refine your skills, improve your techniques, and enhance your understanding of the world around you.

- **Developing Patience**: Treasure hunting requires an incredible amount of patience. Whether you are searching for clues, waiting for a signal from your metal detector, or meticulously planning your next step, the ability to slow down and focus is invaluable. Patience allows you to listen to your instincts, make calculated decisions, and appreciate the journey itself.

- **Story from the Field**: Many treasure hunters recount moments when the real treasure wasn't the object they found, but the peace they discovered in the quiet moments of their search. Some report that the slow process of digging, waiting, and reflecting allowed them to step away from the busyness of life and focus on the present.

B. Critical Thinking and Problem-Solving Skills

- **The Role of Strategy**: The best treasure hunters are also the best strategists. Every treasure hunt involves solving a puzzle. Whether you're interpreting an ancient map, analyzing clues from historical records, or deciphering the meaning behind a cryptic message, the ability to think critically and make quick decisions is key.

- **Navigating Challenges**: Along the way, you'll face new and unexpected challenges. These can be physical obstacles—rugged terrain, inclement weather, or difficult access to remote locations. They can also be intellectual puzzles—trying to figure out the meaning of clues, or encountering unforeseen setbacks in your research. The treasure hunter must become adept at finding solutions quickly, adapting to changes, and overcoming obstacles with ingenuity.

---

2. Building Relationships: The Community of Treasure Hunters

The pursuit of treasure is often seen as a solitary endeavor, with the image of a lone adventurer combing the earth for riches. However, treasure hunting can also be a deeply communal activity. The treasure hunting community is diverse, with members from all walks of life coming together with a shared goal: uncovering hidden history. Along the way, you'll form connections with fellow hunters, local guides, historians, and even strangers who share your passion for discovery.

A. Collaboration and Teamwork

- **The Power of the Team**: Treasure hunting, especially in large or complex quests, often requires a team effort. While one person may be responsible for map analysis, another might be focused on excavation, and yet another might research historical documents. Combining different skill sets can increase your chances of success, as each team member contributes their knowledge and expertise to the quest.

- **Learning from Others**: The treasure hunting community is built on shared knowledge. Whether you're just starting out or you've been hunting for years, learning from others' experiences and mistakes can save you time, money, and frustration. Joining treasure hunting forums, attending meet-ups, or collaborating with experienced hunters can deepen your understanding of the field and expose you to new strategies, tools, and techniques.

- **Building Lasting Friendships**: Many treasure hunters have reported forming deep, lasting friendships as a result of their shared experiences in the field. These relationships often transcend the hunt itself, with people staying in touch long after the treasure has been found. These friendships can be invaluable—offering moral support, shared resources, and a camaraderie that helps you endure the toughest parts of the hunt.

B. Connecting with Local Communities and Histories

- **The Role of Local Knowledge**: Often, locals know more about the treasure you seek than any researcher or historian could. Whether it's an old legend passed down through generations or the location of a forgotten landmark, the knowledge embedded in local culture and community can prove to be the key to unlocking treasure's secrets. Engaging with local communities not only enhances your treasure hunt but also deepens your connection with the history and culture of the place you're exploring.

- **Creating Bonds through History**: Understanding the historical context of your search also helps you connect to the larger narrative. Many treasure hunters report that learning about the people, events, and places associated with the treasure adds a layer of emotional depth to the hunt. It's not just about the wealth—it's about connecting with the past and honoring the lives and stories that came before.

3. Discovering History: Unearthing the Past

Every treasure hunt is a step into the unknown. With each discovery, you don't just uncover material wealth; you uncover pieces of history—stories of lives lived, battles fought, and civilizations risen and fallen. The act of searching for treasure becomes an exploration of the past, a journey into the stories and artifacts that have shaped the present.

A. The Historical Context of Treasure Hunts

- **Unlocking Stories**: When you find an artifact, it's not just an object; it's a link to the past. Whether it's a coin, a shipwreck, or a piece of jewelry, each item holds a story. Who owned it? Where did it come from? What significance did it have? These questions transform a simple object into a rich piece of history.

- **Historical Validation**: As you uncover hidden treasures, you may also unearth pieces of forgotten history. Many treasures were lost over time, and their discovery helps complete the narrative of history. For example, discovering artifacts related to a lost civilization or missing historical figure can shed light on gaps in our understanding of history, providing new perspectives and adding to the historical record.

B. Rediscovering Lost Civilizations and Forgotten Heroes

- **The Personal Connection to History**: Many treasure hunters become emotionally connected to the past as they uncover clues and artifacts. Some develop a personal sense of responsibility for the items they find, seeing themselves as custodians of lost history. They take it upon themselves to protect and preserve these treasures for future generations.

- **Learning About the Past through Treasures**: Whether it's a relic from ancient Rome or an object tied to a famous figure like Amelia Earhart or Pablo Picasso, these items provide a tangible connection to history. Each treasure you uncover brings you closer to understanding the people and events that shaped the world.

4. The Ultimate Treasure: A Life Transformed

At the end of the day, the greatest treasure is not what's hidden beneath the earth or lost in the ocean—it's the way that the treasure hunt transforms you. The journey forces you to evolve as a person, opening up new perspectives, building new relationships, and deepening your connection with the world around you. It is a process of self-discovery and growth, and this journey itself becomes the most significant reward.

A. Re-defining What Wealth Means

- **Beyond Materialism**: As you embark on your treasure hunt, you may find that the wealth you were seeking is not what you imagined it to be. It could be in the friendships you've built, the historical insights you've gained, or the personal strength you've developed. True wealth comes in many forms—often in the intangibles that can't be bought with money.

- **Embracing the Adventure**: Treasure hunting is as much about the adventure as it is about the treasure itself. The experiences, stories, and lessons learned along the way become part of your personal legacy. These intangible treasures are what truly define a rich and fulfilling life.

Chapter 11: The Hidden Treasures of the Mind: How to Unlock Your Greatest Potential

While many treasure hunts focus on the tangible—gold, artifacts, rare collectibles—there is a treasure within each of us that is often overlooked. This chapter will explore the hidden treasures of the mind, the deep well of untapped potential, creativity, and resilience that lie dormant in all human beings. Just as a physical treasure hunt requires exploration, determination, and skill, unlocking the treasures within requires a similar process of self-discovery, discipline, and exploration of the mind.

1. The Power of the Subconscious Mind: Tapping into Hidden Resources

The subconscious mind is an untapped reservoir of knowledge, memories, and instincts that can guide us in profound ways. Just as hidden treasures are waiting to be uncovered beneath the surface of the earth, the subconscious contains treasures waiting to be discovered within us.

A. The Unseen Forces Within Us

- **Understanding the Subconscious**: The subconscious mind stores everything we've ever experienced, every thought we've had, and every emotion we've felt. It is constantly working behind the scenes, influencing our decisions, reactions, and even our beliefs about the world. It holds vast amounts of knowledge that we often don't consciously access. When we learn to tap into this resource, we unlock our hidden potential.

- **Dreams and Intuition**: One of the clearest ways the subconscious communicates with us is through dreams. Often, dreams provide valuable insights, solve problems, or spark creativity. Similarly, our intuition, the gut feeling we often have about situations or people, is the subconscious mind working behind the scenes to process information we may not consciously understand.

- **Practical Application**: Treasure hunters often tap into their intuition when searching for treasure. They learn to trust their instincts when faced with uncertain situations. Similarly, you can begin to train your mind to trust your subconscious. Practice tuning into your inner voice, allowing your intuition to guide you through challenges and new opportunities.

B. Reprogramming Your Mind for Success

- **Overcoming Limiting Beliefs**: Many people carry limiting beliefs—thoughts or fears that hold them back from achieving their true potential. These beliefs, which are often subconscious, tell us that we are not capable, not worthy, or not deserving of success. The first step in unlocking the treasure of your mind is identifying and confronting these beliefs. By reprogramming your mind, you can break free from these barriers and unlock your full potential.

- **Visualization Techniques**: One way to access the treasure within is through visualization. By vividly imagining yourself succeeding, whether in treasure hunting or life goals, you align your conscious and subconscious minds toward achieving those outcomes. Visualization taps into the power of belief, strengthening the mental pathways that can make success inevitable.

- **Affirmations and Positive Thinking**: Reprogramming your subconscious can also be achieved through daily affirmations. Repeating positive statements about yourself and your abilities can help change your self-perception, create new neural pathways, and reshape your subconscious beliefs. This practice is powerful in unlocking the mental treasure that resides within.

2. Creativity: Unlocking the Treasure of Imagination

Creativity is another hidden treasure within all of us. Often, we believe creativity is reserved for artists, musicians, or writers. In reality, creativity is the ability to think outside of the box, to make connections between seemingly unrelated things, and to solve problems in innovative ways. Creativity is not limited to artistic expression—it is the treasure that fuels progress, innovation, and growth.

A. The Role of Imagination in Treasure Hunting

- **Thinking Outside the Box**: In treasure hunting, the ability to think creatively can make the difference between success and failure. Whether it's interpreting an ancient map or finding a hidden clue, creativity allows you to approach problems from new angles and discover solutions that others may have missed.

- **Building New Pathways**: Creativity is essential when facing obstacles. Instead of sticking to one solution, treasure hunters need to build new strategies, reframe old ideas, and think about the problem from a fresh perspective. This is also true in life. The treasure of creativity enables you to break through barriers and discover new ways of thinking and problem-solving.

- **Creative Exercises**: You can strengthen your creativity by practicing exercises that stretch your imagination. These could include brainstorming sessions, drawing, writing, or even playing creative games that challenge you to come up with new ideas. Keeping a journal of creative thoughts or ideas can be an excellent way to train your mind to think outside the box.

B. The Flow State: A Treasure of Productivity and Purpose

- **What is Flow?**: The flow state is a mental state where a person becomes fully immersed and focused on an activity. In this state, time seems to disappear, and the individual feels at their best—both productive and fulfilled. Achieving a flow state is often seen as one of the greatest treasures of the mind because it enables you to tap into your highest levels of creativity, productivity, and focus.

- **Finding Flow in Your Life**: Treasure hunters often experience flow when they are deep into their quest, solving complex clues or overcoming challenges. This sense of immersion is not limited to treasure hunting—it can occur in any activity where your skills and challenges are perfectly balanced. Whether you're working, playing, or learning, seeking and cultivating moments of flow can unlock a deeper sense of fulfillment and joy in your daily life.

- **Cultivating Flow**: To achieve the flow state, it is important to engage in activities that challenge you without overwhelming you. Set clear goals, focus on the task at hand, and eliminate distractions. Practice mindfulness and immerse yourself fully in the experience, allowing your mind to stay present and engaged. This sense of focused attention and purpose will help unlock your potential and increase your productivity.

3. Resilience: The Treasure of Overcoming Adversity

The path to unlocking your potential is not always easy. Just as treasure hunters face adversity in the form of harsh terrain, bad weather, and other obstacles, so too will you encounter setbacks in your personal journey. Resilience—the ability to bounce back from failure, disappointment, and hardship—is one of the greatest treasures you can cultivate.

A. The Strength to Overcome Challenges

- **Embracing Failure as Part of the Process**: Every treasure hunter has faced failure. Whether it's a dead-end lead or a clue that doesn't pan out, failure is part of the process. The key is to view failure not as a sign to give up but as an opportunity to learn and grow. By embracing failure and using it as a stepping stone, you can develop the resilience needed to overcome future challenges.

- **Building Mental Toughness**: Resilience requires mental toughness—an ability to stay focused, remain optimistic, and continue pushing forward despite obstacles. Treasure hunters often develop mental toughness through experience. Similarly, in life, you can build this skill by facing adversity head-on, learning to manage stress, and finding ways to stay positive even when the going gets tough.

B. Developing a Resilient Mindset

- **Positive Reframing**: One of the key elements of resilience is the ability to reframe negative thoughts. Instead of focusing on what went wrong, look at what can be learned from the experience. Reframing challenges as opportunities for growth allows you to stay motivated and keep moving forward.

- **The Power of Gratitude**: Practicing gratitude, even in difficult times, can help you maintain a positive outlook and foster resilience. When faced with challenges, take a moment to reflect on what you have gained from the experience, and what you are thankful for. Gratitude shifts your focus from the obstacles to the opportunities, allowing you to stay emotionally strong.

---

4. Unlocking Your True Potential: The Treasure of Self-Discovery

Ultimately, the treasure hunt of life is about discovering who you truly are. It's about peeling back the layers, confronting the fears and beliefs that hold you back, and stepping into your full potential. The greatest treasure you will ever find is the realization of your own capabilities.

A. The Journey of Self-Discovery

- **Exploring Your Passions and Purpose**: Like a treasure hunt, self-discovery is a journey. It's about uncovering what makes you truly happy, what drives you, and what your deeper purpose is in life. This process can be exhilarating but also challenging. The key is to remain open and curious, allowing yourself to explore different paths and embrace new experiences.

- **Becoming Your Best Self**: As you continue on this journey, you will begin to uncover more about your strengths, weaknesses, and desires. This knowledge becomes the treasure you seek—the wisdom to live a life aligned with your true self.

- **The Role of Mindfulness**: Mindfulness is an essential tool in the journey of self-discovery. By becoming more aware of your thoughts, emotions, and reactions, you can begin to understand the deeper layers of your personality. Practicing mindfulness helps you become more attuned to your inner world, uncovering the hidden treasures of your mind.

Chapter 12: The Treasure of Connection: Building Meaningful Relationships

In the quest for treasure, many focus on material wealth—gold, jewels, rare objects, or riches of some sort. However, there is a treasure far more precious that often goes unappreciated: human connection. This chapter will explore how relationships—whether personal, professional, or communal—represent some of the most valuable treasures we can ever find.

While treasure hunts often emphasize physical wealth, the wealth of meaningful relationships holds the power to enrich every aspect of our lives. Just as a treasure hunt can provide a sense of purpose, drive, and fulfillment, deep, authentic connections with others can bring a sense of belonging, support, and joy that transcends any material pursuit. In this chapter, we will explore how to build, nurture, and cherish the treasures of human connection.

---

1. The Foundation of Connection: Understanding the Value of Relationships

The first step in unlocking the treasure of connection is to understand its value. Relationships are not just about social interactions—they are essential to our well-being, growth, and happiness. Whether through friendships, family, or professional networks, human relationships provide us with support, resources, and opportunities that enrich our lives.

A. The Power of Social Bonds

- **Biological and Emotional Foundations**: Humans are social creatures by nature. From an evolutionary perspective, our survival and success as a species have been built upon our ability to form strong, supportive bonds. These bonds release feel-good chemicals in our brains—oxytocin, dopamine, and serotonin—that make us feel connected, safe, and loved. Social connection is not just an emotional need; it's a biological one.

- **The Impact on Health and Well-being**: Studies have shown that people who maintain strong social connections are healthier, happier, and live longer than those who are isolated. Relationships provide emotional support, reduce stress, and contribute to our mental and physical health. In fact, the importance of relationships can be likened to other foundational treasures, like wealth, because they impact every facet of life.

- **Application in Treasure Hunting**: Treasure hunters know that the success of their journey often depends on collaboration. They rely on the support and expertise of others to uncover hidden riches. Likewise, in life, building meaningful connections with people who share similar values, goals, or interests can create a support system that helps us overcome challenges and reach our own version of success.

B. The Treasure of Family Bonds

- **The First Connection**: For many, family is the first treasure trove of connection we ever experience. Family provides a sense of identity, continuity, and security, and these bonds are often the most lasting in our lives. While family dynamics can sometimes be complex or challenging, the foundation of love and loyalty within families can become one of the most meaningful treasures of all.

- **Healing and Strength in Family**: Families are unique in their ability to offer both unconditional love and, at times, unconditional conflict. However, it is within these relationships that we learn the greatest lessons about resilience, forgiveness, and personal growth. A family can serve as a pillar of strength through times of hardship and provide an essential anchor to the storms of life.

- **Preserving Family Bonds**: Just as treasure hunters guard their discoveries carefully, it is essential to nurture and preserve family bonds. This means prioritizing communication, making time for each other, and practicing empathy. The treasure found in family connection is not always easy to maintain but is always worth the effort.

2. The Treasure of Friendships: Building Deep, Lasting Relationships

While family connections are crucial, friendships offer a unique kind of treasure. Friends provide companionship, shared experiences, and mutual support that contribute to a fulfilling life. The depth of friendship is often measured not by the number of people you know, but by the quality of those relationships.

A. The Richness of True Friendship

- **Shared Joys and Sorrows**: True friendships are built on shared experiences—both the happy moments and the difficult times. These bonds are not superficial; they are forged through trust, vulnerability, and mutual understanding. A true friend is someone who knows your strengths and weaknesses, supports you through challenges, and celebrates your successes.

- **The Role of Empathy and Compassion**: Like treasure hunters relying on each other's skills and strengths, friendships thrive on empathy and compassion. Friends who listen, offer advice, and provide emotional support are treasures that enrich our lives in ways that no material wealth can match.

- **Building Meaningful Friendships**: Meaningful friendships require effort and authenticity. Investing time in getting to know others, being present in their lives, and being vulnerable with them creates a treasure trove of trust and intimacy. Friendship is not transactional—it is a mutual exchange of care, respect, and love.

- **Quality over Quantity**: Just as treasure hunters focus on finding the right clues, not every relationship is meant to be deep or lasting. It's important to focus on building a small circle of true friends rather than spreading yourself thin with superficial acquaintances. The quality of your relationships will bring more treasure to your life than the quantity of people you know.

B. The Bonds of Professional Networks: Leveraging Connections for Growth

While personal connections often dominate discussions of relationship treasures, professional relationships are an equally important part of the treasure map of life. Business and career success can often be enhanced by building strategic relationships within your industry or community. A professional network offers access to resources, knowledge, opportunities, and guidance.

- **Networking with Purpose**: Professional relationships are not simply about collecting business cards or making contacts for the sake of it. The true treasure lies in forming authentic, mutually beneficial connections. Take the time to get to know people, offer help and support, and build relationships grounded in trust and respect.

- **Mentorship: The Golden Key to Success**: Mentorship is one of the greatest treasures in a professional network. A mentor offers guidance, advice, and experience that can help you navigate challenges, refine your skills, and advance your career. Finding a mentor and being a mentor to others can create a valuable cycle of growth and success.

- **Fostering Collaboration**: Just as treasure hunters often form teams to tackle difficult quests, collaborating with others in the professional realm leads to greater innovation, shared resources, and expanded opportunities. Building relationships within your industry can lead to partnerships, joint ventures, and opportunities that would otherwise remain out of reach.

3. The Treasure of Community: Building Connections that Lift Us All

One of the greatest treasures we can uncover is the sense of connection to a larger community. While individual relationships are valuable, the treasure of belonging to a group, a cause, or a shared purpose creates a powerful sense of fulfillment and meaning. Communities—whether local or global—allow us to contribute, learn, grow, and thrive as part of something greater than ourselves.

A. The Gift of Shared Purpose

- **Purpose Beyond the Self**: A community gives us a sense of belonging, a place where we can contribute to a shared purpose. Whether it's through volunteer work, participating in a social cause, or being part of a local or global initiative, community offers a deep sense of meaning that can't be found in isolation.

- **The Strength of Collective Action**: When individuals come together as part of a group, their collective power is far greater than the sum of their parts. Communities offer a treasure trove of knowledge, resources, and support that enables individuals to achieve goals they would not be able to accomplish alone.

- **Engaging with Community**: Getting involved in your community is one of the most rewarding investments you can make. Seek out opportunities to connect with others, offer your time and skills, and learn from those around you. The wealth of community is far richer than material wealth because it nurtures our deeper human need for connection, contribution, and belonging.

4. The Treasure of Love: The Ultimate Connection

Ultimately, love represents the most profound and enduring form of connection. The love between romantic partners, between parents and children, and the love that unites people across all walks of life is the ultimate treasure of human existence. It is the treasure that transcends all others, offering a sense of belonging, fulfillment, and joy that cannot be surpassed.

A. The Many Forms of Love

- **Romantic Love**: The love between partners is one of the most celebrated and cherished forms of human connection. It provides intimacy, passion, companionship, and a deep sense of shared life. This love, when nurtured with care, grows deeper over time, becoming a treasure that lasts a lifetime.

- **Familial Love**: The love between parents and children, siblings, and extended family members forms the foundation of human connection. This love provides security, comfort, and support, helping us navigate life's challenges.

- **Unconditional Love**: The purest form of love is often unconditional—a love that doesn't depend on actions or outcomes but exists simply because of who we are. This love is a treasure that allows us to grow and evolve without judgment, creating an environment where we feel safe and supported.

Chapter 13: The Treasure of Knowledge: Unlocking the Wisdom of the Ages

In every treasure hunt, the key to discovery lies not just in the physical items you find, but in the knowledge and wisdom you acquire along the way. This chapter delves into the treasure of knowledge—understanding how knowledge, whether academic, experiential, or intuitive, can open doors to new opportunities, solve complex problems, and enrich our lives in ways beyond measure. Much like a treasure hunter who studies maps, deciphers clues, and learns from others' experiences, we too must recognize the value of knowledge in guiding us to life's true treasures.

---

1. The Value of Knowledge: More Than a Tool—A Treasure

At its core, knowledge is a powerful tool, but its value extends far beyond that. Knowledge is the foundation for growth, transformation, and innovation. It enables us to understand the world around us, make informed decisions, and navigate challenges with confidence. From ancient wisdom passed down through generations to cutting-edge scientific discoveries, knowledge is a treasure that grows in value with time, use, and exploration.

A. Knowledge as a Compass

- **Navigating Life's Challenges**: Knowledge serves as a compass to navigate life's complexities, much like a treasure hunter uses a map to locate hidden riches. Whether it's the wisdom of ancestors or the latest insights in technology, knowledge equips us with the tools needed to face the unknown and make sense of our circumstances. It helps us find our way through difficult situations, and just as importantly, it guides us toward opportunities that we might have otherwise missed.

- **The Search for Truth**: Knowledge provides us with a path to uncover truths that are often hidden in plain sight. For centuries, people have searched for treasures both physical and intellectual, but often the most valuable treasures are those that illuminate the hidden realities of our lives. As we dig deeper into various areas of knowledge—whether historical, philosophical, scientific, or spiritual—we unlock deeper layers of truth that shape our understanding of the world and ourselves.

B. Types of Knowledge: From Academic to Experiential

Not all knowledge is the same. There are various types of knowledge that contribute to our wealth of understanding, each offering a unique set of benefits.

- **Academic Knowledge**: This refers to formal, structured learning gained through education, study, and research. It encompasses a wide range of subjects, from literature and history to mathematics and science. Academic knowledge forms the foundation for many of the modern discoveries that propel us forward, but it also helps us make sense of past civilizations, the evolution of thought, and the framework of the world we live in today.

  - **The Pursuit of Expertise**: True mastery in a field is akin to finding a treasure chest full of expertise. To excel in any domain—whether medicine, law, engineering, or the arts—requires dedicated learning and an accumulation of knowledge over time. This expertise becomes a powerful asset that opens doors to new opportunities and enhances our ability to contribute meaningfully to society.

- **Experiential Knowledge**: While academic knowledge is crucial, experiential knowledge—the kind of wisdom that comes from lived experience—often holds just as much, if not more, value. Through trial and error, personal growth, and the lessons learned from successes and failures, we acquire a deep understanding of how the world works, how people behave, and how we can navigate the complexities of life.

  - **Learning from Life's Treasure Map**: Each person's life is a unique treasure map, filled with experiences and lessons that cannot be replicated. Experiential knowledge is invaluable in guiding us through the ups and downs of life. It teaches resilience, adaptability, and the ability to face adversity with courage. This form of knowledge is often the richest and most rewarding because it shapes our character, perspective, and approach to life's challenges.

- **Intuitive Knowledge**: Intuition is often referred to as "gut feeling" or "inner wisdom." It's the ability to understand something instinctively, without the need for conscious reasoning. While it may not be based on hard facts or formal education, intuitive knowledge is a deeply valuable asset. In many ways, it serves as an internal compass, guiding us when logic and reason fall short.

  - **Trusting Your Inner Compass**: As we venture through life's treasure hunt, sometimes the greatest discoveries come from listening to our intuition. Trusting our instincts helps us make decisions in moments of uncertainty, allowing us to move forward when external data and analysis aren't available. Intuitive knowledge may not always be easy to define, but its impact can be profound in guiding us toward the right path.

2. The Treasure of Lifelong Learning: Constant Growth and Exploration

One of the most powerful ways to access the treasure of knowledge is through lifelong learning. This is the ongoing, voluntary, and self-motivated pursuit of knowledge for personal or professional development. Much like a treasure hunter who continually refines their skills and seeks new clues, we too must remain committed to exploring new fields, acquiring new skills, and challenging our existing knowledge.

A. Cultivating a Growth Mindset

- **The Power of Curiosity**: At the heart of lifelong learning is curiosity. When we maintain a sense of wonder about the world, we remain open to new ideas, perspectives, and opportunities. Curiosity leads us to ask questions, seek answers, and venture into new areas of discovery. It's this curiosity that drives the treasure hunt of life, pushing us to explore, experiment, and continuously learn.

- **Embracing Challenges**: Lifelong learning requires us to embrace challenges as opportunities for growth. Just as a treasure hunter may encounter difficult terrain or unexpected setbacks, we too will face obstacles in our journey of knowledge acquisition. A growth mindset allows us to see these obstacles not as barriers, but as stepping stones to greater understanding. By reframing challenges as learning experiences, we unlock even more treasures along the way.

B. The Role of Technology in Unlocking Knowledge

- **Digital Resources**: In today's digital age, knowledge is more accessible than ever before. The internet, online courses, digital libraries, and social media platforms have revolutionized the way we learn. Anyone with an internet connection can access an endless pool of knowledge— whether it's learning a new language, mastering a new skill, or understanding the complexities of the universe.

- **Artificial Intelligence and Knowledge Expansion**: As technology advances, artificial intelligence (AI) and machine learning are beginning to revolutionize the way we acquire and process knowledge. AI can analyze vast amounts of data, uncover patterns, and offer insights that humans may have missed. By leveraging these technologies, we can accelerate our understanding of complex topics and uncover new treasures of knowledge that would otherwise be inaccessible.

3. The Treasure of History: Learning from the Past

History is a treasure chest of lessons, mistakes, triumphs, and discoveries. By studying the past, we not only gain insight into the actions and decisions that shaped our world but also uncover timeless wisdom that can guide us in the present.

A. Understanding Our Roots

- **The Wisdom of Ancient Civilizations**: From the Egyptians to the Greeks, Romans, and beyond, ancient civilizations have left us a wealth of knowledge that continues to influence our lives today. By studying history, we can understand the values, beliefs, and innovations that shaped human culture. This understanding can provide us with perspective, wisdom, and guidance for navigating the present.

- **Learning from Mistakes**: History is not just a collection of achievements; it's also a record of mistakes, wars, and injustices. By studying these aspects of history, we gain insight into how we can avoid repeating past errors and create a more just, peaceful, and prosperous future.

B. History as a Source of Inspiration

- **The Lessons of Resilience**: The stories of individuals and societies that have overcome adversity can be incredibly inspiring. These examples serve as reminders that even in the face of seemingly insurmountable obstacles, human ingenuity, determination, and resilience can lead to breakthroughs and triumphs. Whether it's the story of a great leader, an inventor, or a revolutionary, history provides a roadmap of how we can face our own challenges with courage and creativity.

4. The Treasure of Learning from Others: Mentors and Guides

While personal knowledge is invaluable, the knowledge and guidance we gain from others can provide us with shortcuts to success and help us avoid common pitfalls. Mentors, teachers, and guides offer wisdom that accelerates our growth and allows us to access treasures of knowledge we may not have discovered on our own.

A. The Value of Mentorship

- **Finding the Right Guide**: Just as a treasure hunter would never embark on a quest without the guidance of an expert, we too need mentors who can provide us with insights and advice. A mentor can offer perspective, challenge our thinking, and help us unlock our true potential. The treasure of mentorship is the transfer of wisdom and experience from someone who has already walked the path we wish to follow.

- **Becoming a Mentor**: As we acquire knowledge, we too can become mentors for others. Sharing our wisdom, experience, and guidance not only helps others find their own treasures, but it also reinforces our own learning and growth. The act of teaching and mentoring creates a cycle of knowledge that benefits both the mentor and the mentee.

Chapter 14: The Hidden Treasures of the Mind: Unlocking Mental Wealth

In the quest for riches, many people overlook the most valuable treasure of all: the power of the mind. This chapter explores how our mental landscape is not only the source of our knowledge and creativity but also the key to unlocking untapped potential that can lead to extraordinary wealth in both tangible and intangible forms. Just as a treasure hunter carefully studies a map to uncover hidden gems, we must learn to navigate and unlock the treasures within our own minds.

---

1. The Power of Mental Wealth: Your Greatest Hidden Treasure

The mind is an incredible treasure chest, one that often goes unnoticed or underutilized in our pursuit of external wealth. In fact, the wealth we possess mentally and emotionally may far exceed any material treasure we might seek. Our thoughts, beliefs, perceptions, and abilities form the foundation of who we are and what we can achieve. By investing in the development of our minds, we unlock a treasure trove of possibilities that can change the course of our lives.

A. Understanding Mental Wealth

- **More Than Just Knowledge**: Mental wealth is not limited to the accumulation of facts or data. It includes emotional intelligence, creativity, adaptability, and the power of imagination. Mental wealth is the ability to think critically, solve problems, and build lasting relationships. It's a vast, ever-expanding storehouse of potential that we can tap into at any point in our lives.

- **The Wealth of Self-Discovery**: The first step in unlocking your mental treasure is discovering who you truly are. By delving deep into your own thoughts, fears, dreams, and desires, you begin to uncover the potential that lies hidden beneath the surface. Self-awareness is the foundation upon which all other mental wealth is built. The more we understand about ourselves, the more we can shape our lives in alignment with our deepest values and aspirations.

- **Beliefs and Mindset**: One of the most powerful aspects of mental wealth is the ability to shape our own beliefs. Our mindset determines how we perceive the world and respond to challenges. A fixed mindset can limit our potential, while a growth mindset empowers us to embrace challenges as opportunities for growth. By changing our mindset, we can transform how we approach life's challenges, turning them into stepping stones to success.

B. Cultivating Mental Wealth Through Focus and Discipline

- **The Role of Focus**: Just as a treasure hunter needs to stay focused on the goal despite distractions, we too must train our minds to focus on the important tasks at hand. Focus is essential in unlocking our mental treasures because it enables us to channel our energy into the right areas, whether it's learning new skills, pursuing creative ideas, or solving complex problems. A focused mind is one that is not easily swayed by external noise or internal distractions but is laser-focused on the path to success.

- **Developing Mental Discipline**: Discipline is another cornerstone of mental wealth. It's the ability to stay committed to our goals even when the journey gets tough.

Mental discipline is about forming good habits, staying consistent in our efforts, and making intentional choices that support our long-term vision. Whether it's sticking to a study routine, practicing mindfulness, or dedicating time to a creative project, mental discipline ensures that we remain on track and continue moving toward our goals.

2. The Treasure of Emotional Intelligence: Mastering Your Emotions

Emotional intelligence (EQ) is often regarded as one of the most valuable forms of mental wealth. It's the ability to understand, control, and express our emotions, as well as the ability to recognize and influence the emotions of others. High EQ is linked to greater success in both personal and professional settings because it helps us navigate social complexities, build meaningful relationships, and manage stress effectively. Emotional intelligence is a treasure that can lead to a richer, more fulfilling life.

A. Understanding Emotional Intelligence

- **Self-Awareness**: At the heart of emotional intelligence is self-awareness—the ability to recognize and understand our own emotions. Self-aware individuals are more in tune with their feelings and can respond to situations in a way that aligns with their values. They are aware of how their emotions affect their decisions and interactions with others.

- **Self-Regulation**: Once we understand our emotions, the next step is to manage them effectively. Emotional regulation means having control over how we respond to our emotions, especially in stressful or challenging situations. It's about pausing before reacting, choosing our responses thoughtfully, and maintaining composure under pressure.

- **Empathy and Social Awareness**: High EQ also involves empathy—the ability to understand and share the feelings of others. Empathy fosters deeper connections with people, making us better communicators and more supportive friends, colleagues, and partners. Social awareness is about recognizing the emotional dynamics in a group setting, understanding the needs and concerns of others, and responding appropriately to different situations.

- **Building Relationships**: Emotional intelligence is a critical asset for building lasting, meaningful relationships. Whether it's in our personal lives or at work, the ability to connect with others on an emotional level helps foster trust, collaboration, and mutual respect. Building strong relationships is akin to finding a hidden treasure—one that provides lasting value and enriches our lives in countless ways.

3. Creative Potential: The Treasure of Innovation and Imagination

Creativity is another powerful form of mental wealth. It's the ability to think outside the box, generate new ideas, and approach problems from innovative angles. Creativity is often the key to unlocking solutions to challenges, whether they are in business, art, or personal life. Those who are able to harness their creative potential often find that the treasures they uncover are the most rewarding.

A. Unlocking Creative Flow

- **The Importance of Play**: Just as treasure hunters often take time to relax and reflect during their journeys, creativity thrives in an environment of play and exploration. Allowing our minds to wander, experiment, and explore new ideas without judgment opens the door to creative insights. Playfulness encourages the brain to form new connections, fostering innovative thinking and problem-solving.

- **Overcoming Creative Blocks**: Every treasure hunt has its obstacles, and so does the process of creativity. Sometimes, we face creative blocks that prevent us from moving forward. The key to overcoming these blocks is persistence. By continuing to engage with our creative process, trying new approaches, and seeking inspiration from various sources, we eventually uncover new ideas and solutions.

- **Collaborative Creativity**: While individual creativity is valuable, collaborating with others can amplify creative potential. Group brainstorming sessions, creative partnerships, and diverse teams bring different perspectives and ideas to the table, often leading to groundbreaking innovations. Just as a treasure hunter may rely on a team for skills and insights, so too can creative minds benefit from collaboration.

4. Mental Fitness: Strengthening Your Brain for Lifelong Success

Just as we must train our bodies to maintain physical health, mental fitness requires regular exercise to maintain peak performance. Mental fitness involves activities that enhance cognitive abilities, improve focus, and increase mental resilience. These exercises help keep our brains sharp, flexible, and ready to tackle new challenges.

A. Brain Exercises for Mental Clarity

- **Mindfulness and Meditation**: One of the most powerful tools for improving mental fitness is mindfulness and meditation. These practices help to calm the mind, reduce stress, and improve focus. By regularly engaging in mindfulness exercises, we train our minds to stay present, which leads to greater clarity, creativity, and emotional balance.

- **Cognitive Challenges**: Just as physical exercise strengthens the body, cognitive challenges—such as puzzles, games, and learning new skills—help strengthen the brain. Engaging in activities that challenge our cognitive abilities promotes neuroplasticity, the brain's ability to form new neural connections. This means that we can continually grow our mental capacity, just like we would develop physical muscle through exercise.

5. The Treasure of Mental Resilience: Overcoming Adversity

One of the most valuable aspects of mental wealth is resilience—the ability to bounce back from adversity. Life will inevitably present challenges, whether in the form of personal loss, professional setbacks, or external crises. Mental resilience is the treasure that allows us to face adversity head-on, learn from our experiences, and continue moving forward.

A. Building Mental Toughness

- **Adapting to Change**: The world is constantly changing, and resilience allows us to adapt to these changes without being overwhelmed. Whether it's adapting to a new job, a change in circumstances, or an unexpected crisis, resilient individuals have the ability to stay calm, assess the situation, and take effective action.

- **Learning from Failure**: Resilience is not about avoiding failure, but about learning from it. Every failure contains valuable lessons that can propel us toward success. The treasure lies in our ability to extract those lessons and apply them to future endeavors.

Chapter 15: The Legacy of Treasure: Leaving a Lasting Impact

As the final chapter of our journey into the treasure of life, we turn our attention to a concept that transcends the accumulation of material wealth: legacy. Treasure is not simply about what we find or acquire; it's about what we leave behind. The impact we have on others, the mark we make on the world, and the way we choose to use our resources to enrich others is the true treasure that endures long after we are gone.

In this chapter, we explore how creating a lasting legacy is the ultimate treasure—a treasure that grows in value over time and benefits not only ourselves but future generations. As we uncover the treasure inside, we are reminded that the riches we amass during our lifetime are best used to inspire, empower, and support the greater good.

1. Defining Legacy: What Are You Leaving Behind?

A legacy is more than just a collection of wealth, assets, or accomplishments. It's the unique mark we leave on the world, the imprint of who we are, and the influence we have on those around us. It is the essence of how we are remembered and how our contributions are woven into the fabric of history.

A. The Components of Legacy

- **Family and Relationships**: One of the most important aspects of our legacy is the love, support, and guidance we provide to our families and communities. The way we nurture relationships, raise children, mentor others, and build communities forms the foundation of a lasting legacy. It's about ensuring that our values, wisdom, and love are passed down and carried forward.

- **Career and Accomplishments**: While career achievements are often visible, the true impact of our work is measured by how it affects others. Whether through innovation, leadership, or creative endeavors, the work we do can serve as a testament to our abilities and the difference we make in the world.

- **Acts of Kindness and Giving Back**: A legacy is often shaped by acts of kindness, charity, and generosity. The treasures we share with others—whether it's our time, resources, knowledge, or compassion—are invaluable.

These acts may seem small at the time but often grow into monumental impacts that ripple through generations.

- **Cultural and Social Contributions**: Many people's legacies are marked by their contributions to culture, art, social justice, and progress. Pioneers in various fields—science, art, politics, and human rights—leave behind a legacy that continues to inspire and shape the future.

B. Building a Meaningful Legacy

Creating a meaningful legacy involves intentionality. Just as a treasure hunter carefully plans each step of their journey, we must actively choose how we want to be remembered and what impact we want to have on the world. This process involves self-reflection, values assessment, and conscious decision-making about how to live a life that will leave an enduring mark.

- **Start with Your Values**: At the heart of any lasting legacy is a foundation built on strong values. Ask yourself: What principles do I stand by? What causes do I care most about? How do I want my actions to align with my beliefs? These values will guide every decision you make and help you build a legacy that truly reflects who you are.

- **Set Long-Term Goals**: A meaningful legacy doesn't happen overnight. It's the result of consistent, long-term effort. Take the time to set goals that will allow you to leave an impact, whether through mentoring, giving, or creating work that will outlast your lifetime. Remember, the journey to a great legacy is just as important as the destination.

- **Be Intentional with Time and Resources**: Legacy requires an investment of time, energy, and resources. It's not just about wealth but how we choose to use that wealth, time, and influence to make a difference in the lives of others. Whether it's funding a cause, dedicating time to helping others, or making sacrifices for the greater good, intentionality ensures that your treasure is spent in ways that will continue to benefit others long after you're gone.

2. The Role of Mentorship: Passing the Torch

One of the most profound ways to leave a legacy is by mentoring others. Mentorship isn't about simply teaching someone a skill or giving advice—it's about nurturing growth, inspiring potential, and providing the guidance that helps others reach their full potential.

A. The Power of Mentorship

Mentorship serves as a transfer of knowledge, wisdom, and life lessons from one individual to another. As mentors, we pass on our experiences, perspectives, and understanding of the world, allowing those we mentor to build upon our insights and create their own path.

- **Impact Beyond the Individual**: The beauty of mentorship lies in its ability to ripple out. When you help someone reach their potential, you not only change their life but also influence the lives of everyone they come into contact with. A mentor's legacy is multiplied as the mentee grows and continues to pass on the lessons they've learned to others.

- **Long-Term Influence**: Unlike material wealth, which can be spent or lost, the knowledge, confidence, and opportunities passed through mentorship can continue to impact generations. By investing in the growth of others, you plant seeds of success that grow long after you are gone.

---

3. Philanthropy and Giving: Sharing the Treasure

Philanthropy is another powerful way to create a lasting legacy. The wealth we accumulate during our lives holds the potential to make a profound difference when used for the benefit of others. This can range from financial donations to charitable organizations, to supporting local communities, to funding scholarships and research. Philanthropy transforms wealth into a force for good, leaving an enduring legacy of care, compassion, and social change.

A. The Joy of Giving Back

Giving is one of the purest expressions of legacy. When we share our resources, whether it's money, time, or expertise, we help solve problems, address injustices, and improve lives. The more we give, the more our legacy expands, becoming a gift that continues to give.

- **The Ripple Effect of Giving**: Each act of generosity creates a ripple effect. One donation or act of kindness can lead to more donations and more kindness, multiplying the impact far beyond what we could have imagined. Every penny, every hour, and every word of encouragement invested in others becomes part of a greater legacy.

- **Philanthropy as a Path to Personal Fulfillment**: Many people find that giving back is not only a way to leave a lasting legacy but also a source of personal fulfillment. The joy and satisfaction that come from knowing your actions have had a positive impact on others are treasures in themselves.

---

4. Preserving Your Legacy for Future Generations

To ensure that your legacy endures, it's important to plan for the future. This involves not only documenting your achievements and passing on your values but also making strategic decisions about how your resources and wisdom will be shared with future generations.

A. Creating a Will and Estate Plan

While the thought of planning for the end of life can feel uncomfortable, it's essential for ensuring that your material wealth and personal legacy are passed on according to your wishes. This may involve creating a will, establishing trusts, or setting up charitable foundations that carry on your values.

- **Legacy Letters and Documents**: In addition to material assets, consider writing legacy letters—personal messages for your children, grandchildren, or loved ones that share your values, stories, and life lessons. These documents help future generations understand the legacy you've created and how they can continue it.

- **Investing in Education and Scholarships**: Many individuals choose to create scholarships or educational programs as a way to invest in the future. By supporting the education of others, you help ensure that the knowledge, skills, and wisdom you've developed are passed down, furthering the legacy of growth and achievement.

---

5. The Eternal Treasure: A Life Well-Lived

At the end of the day, the most valuable legacy we leave behind is the example we set for others. The way we live our lives— how we treat others, how we overcome adversity, and how we choose to make the world a better place—is the greatest treasure we can offer. A life well-lived, grounded in integrity, kindness, and purpose, becomes the ultimate treasure.

The journey to a lasting legacy is about embracing the beauty of life's treasure hunt, recognizing that the richest treasures lie not in what we acquire but in the lives we touch and the positive changes we inspire. As you continue your own treasure hunt through life, remember: the true treasure is not what we collect, but what we give away.

Conclusion: Uncovering the True Treasure Within

As we close this journey through "There's Treasure Inside," it becomes clear that the greatest treasure we will ever find is not a chest full of gold or jewels, but the richness of life itself. It is the treasure of personal growth, the impact we have on the world, and the love and wisdom we share with others. The treasure hunt we embark upon is not one of physical discovery, but of unlocking the immense potential that lies within each of us.

Throughout this book, we've explored how wealth comes in many forms—financial, yes, but also intellectual, emotional, and spiritual. The true treasure is found not in the accumulation of material possessions, but in how we choose to live, the values we uphold, and the way we enrich the lives of others. The ultimate purpose of this treasure hunt is to discover the depth of our own lives and the profound impact we can have on the world.

In the chapters before us, we've uncovered the treasures hidden in our relationships, careers, acts of kindness, and the legacy we leave. Each of these elements contributes to the larger tapestry of who we are, and by nurturing them, we are building a legacy far greater than any single material possession. The treasure is not something we collect—it is something we give, share, and pass on.

The call to action that we leave with you is simple: **Take the treasure hunt seriously, but remember that the treasure is already inside you**. It is in your actions, in your choices, in the way you interact with others, and in the mark you leave on the world. True treasure grows richer the more it is shared and multiplied.

Whether or not you set out to find the literal treasures scattered across America, the journey of self-discovery and self-realization is the most valuable treasure of all. As you continue your own adventure through life, remember that **the greatest treasures you can unearth are not buried in the earth—but are inside you, waiting to be discovered, shared, and passed down for generations to come**.

In the end, **there's treasure inside you**—and it's a treasure more valuable than any gold, jewel, or artifact. It's a treasure of impact, love, kindness, wisdom, and legacy. What you do with it will determine the course of your life and the mark you leave on the world. So, go forth with the knowledge that your treasure hunt is far from over—it's just begun.

And as you uncover more treasures along the way, remember that the ultimate treasure is found in the journey itself, the lives you touch, and the legacy you leave behind.

Made in the USA
Las Vegas, NV
03 December 2024